REALLY
Writing Workbook

FOR 5 YEAR OLDS

This book belongs to...

Contributers: Under licence from Shutterstock
ISBN 978-1-912155-77-4

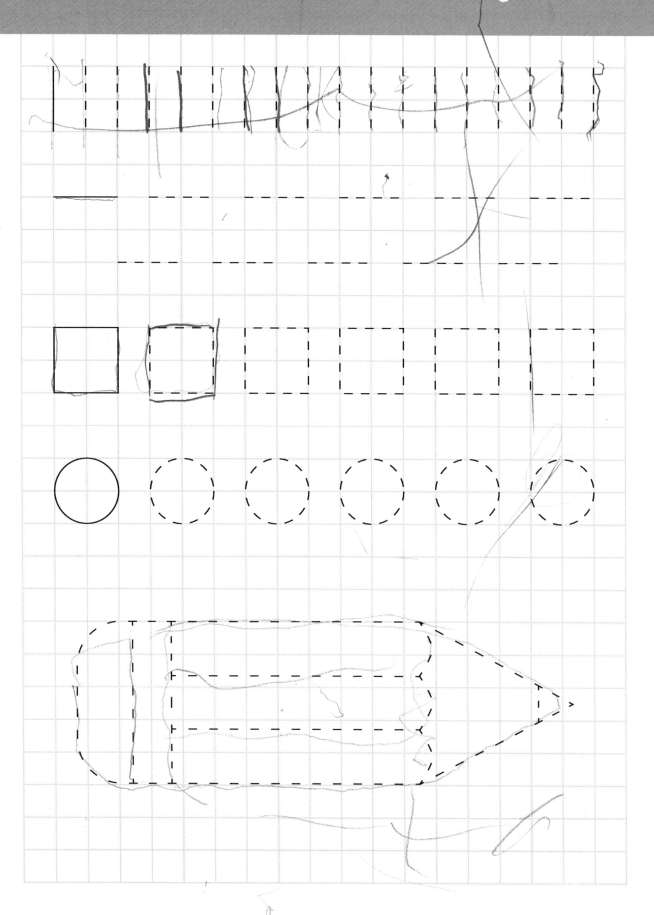

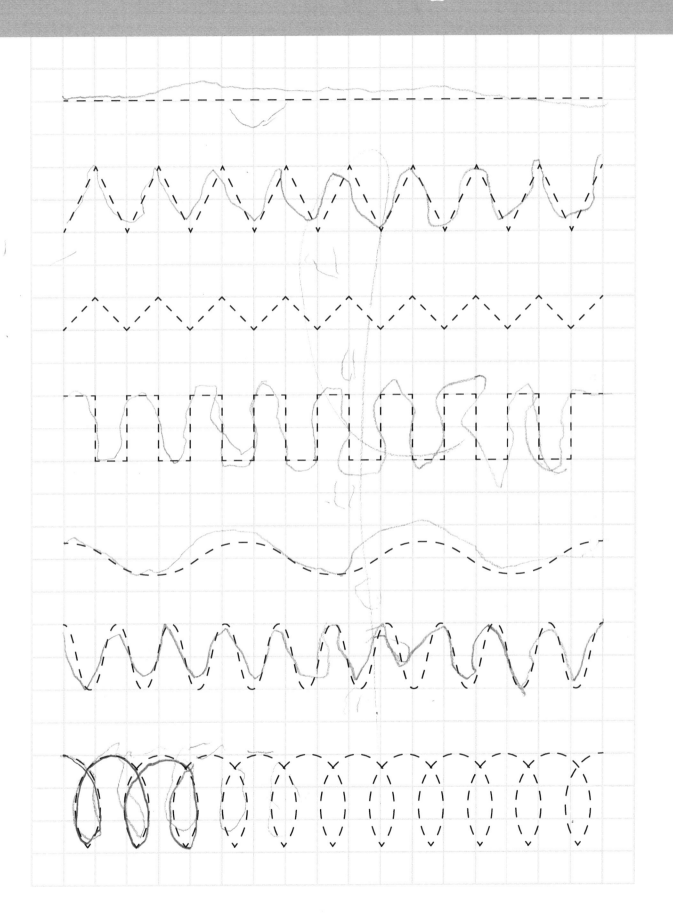

Carefully trace & practice

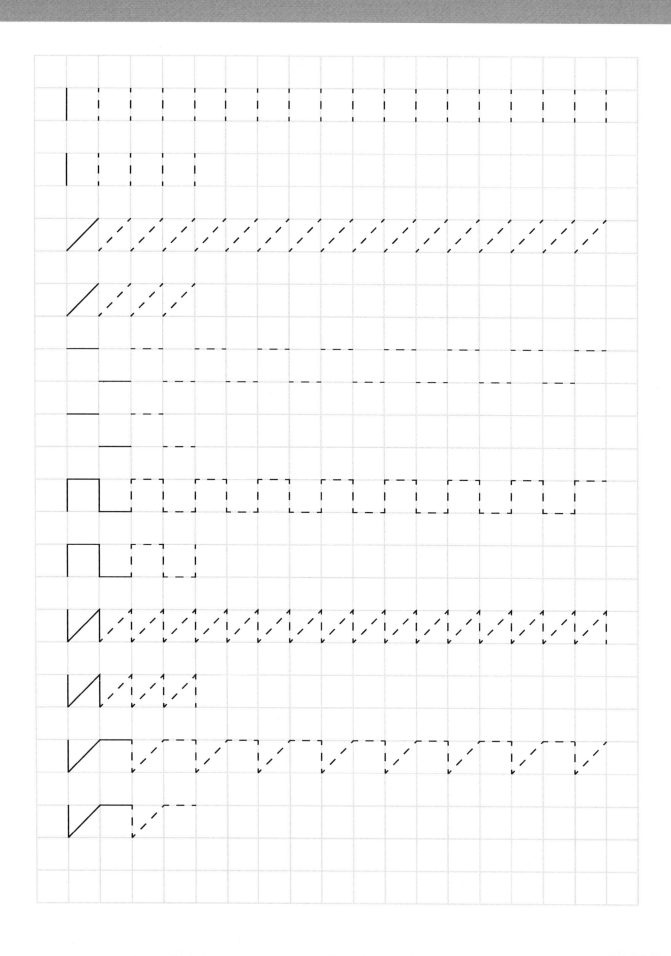

Aa

Apple

AAAAAAA

aaaaaaa

Bb

Butterfly

BBBBBBBB

bbbbbbbb

C c   C c

Cake

c c c c c c c

c c c c c c c c

Dd

Dd

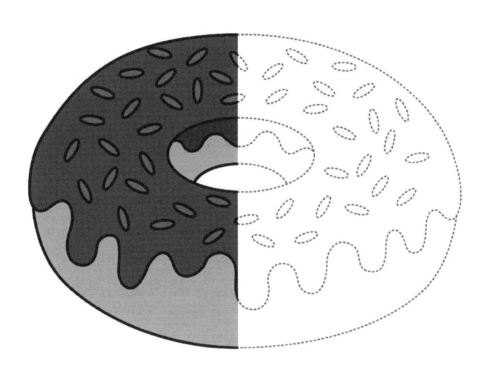

Donut

DDDDDDD

ddddddd

E e

Ee

Easter egg

EEEEEEEE

eeeeeeeee

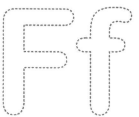

Ff

Ff

fish

F F F F F F F

f f f f f f f f f

Gg

Gift

G G G G G G

g g g g g g g

Hh

House

HHHHHHHHH

hhhhhhhhhh

practice

Ii

Ii

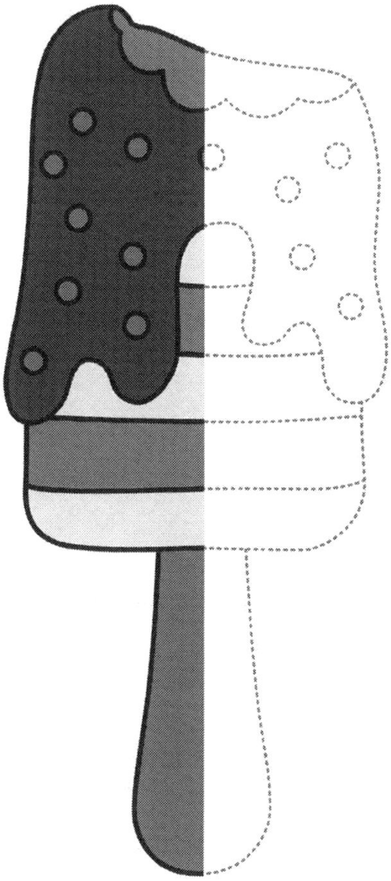

Ice cream

I I I I I I I I I

i i i i i i i i i i i i

Jj

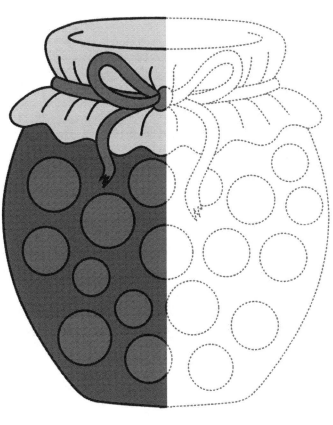

J j

Jam

JJJJJJJ

j j j j j j j j j j j

Kk

Kk

Key

KKKKKKKK

kkkkkkkkk

Ll

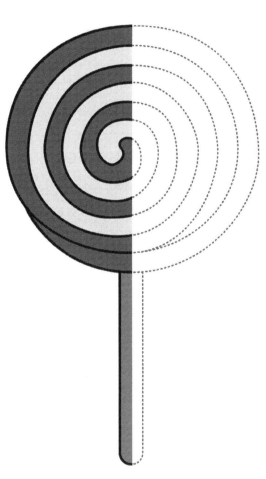

Ll

Lollipop

Mm

Mushroom

MMMMMM

mmmmmm

Nn

Nn

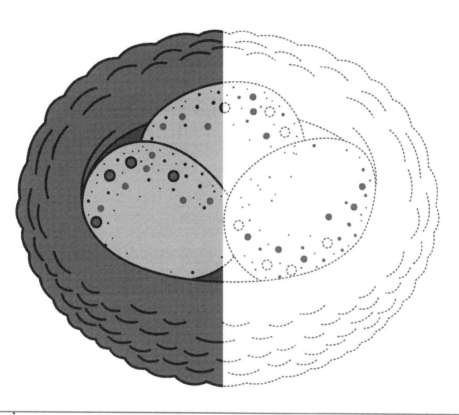

Nest

NNNNNNN

nnnnnnnn

O o   O o

Owl

P p

Pencil

PPPPPPPP

ppppppppp

Qq

Qq

Queen

QQQQQQQQ

qqqqqqqqqq

R r

R r

Rainbow

RRRRRRRR

rrrrrrrr

S s   S s

Sun

SSSSSSS

SSSSSSS

Tt

Tt

Teapot

TTTTTTT

tttttttttt

Uu   Uu

Umbrella

UUUUUUUU

uuuuuuuuu

Vv

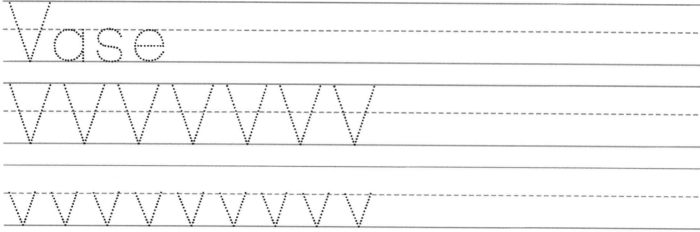

Vase

Ww

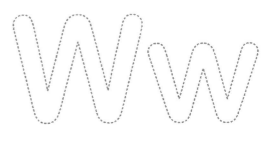

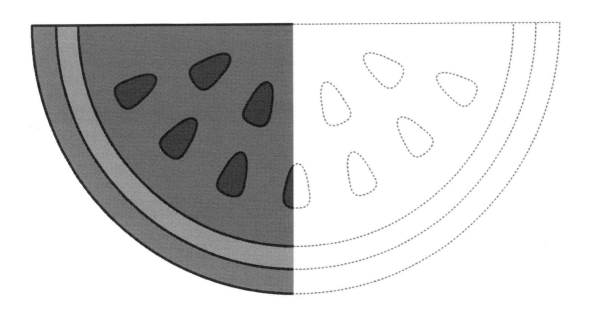

Watermelon

WWWWWW

wwwwww

Xx

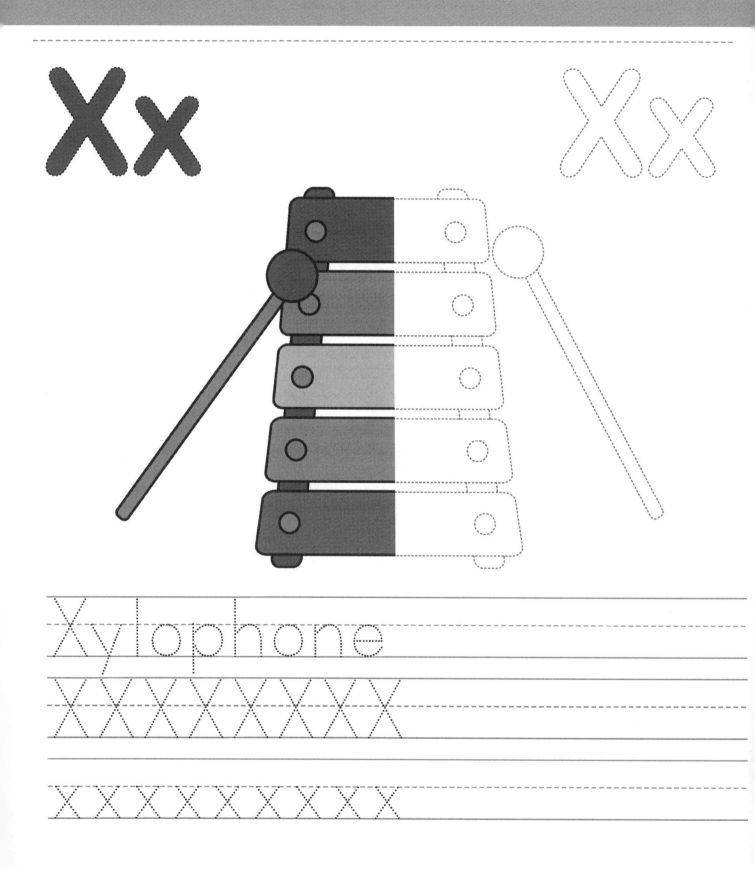

Xylophone

XXXXXXXX

XXXXXXXXX

Yy

Yarn

Y Y Y Y Y Y Y Y

y y y y y y y y

Z z

Z z

Zebra

Z Z Z Z Z Z Z

Z Z Z Z Z Z Z

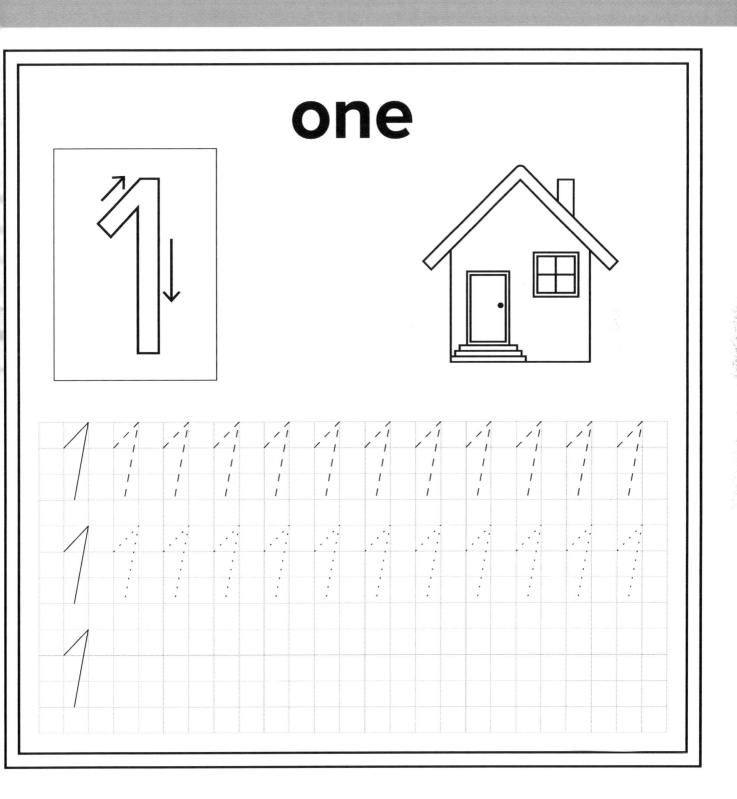

one

How many houses?

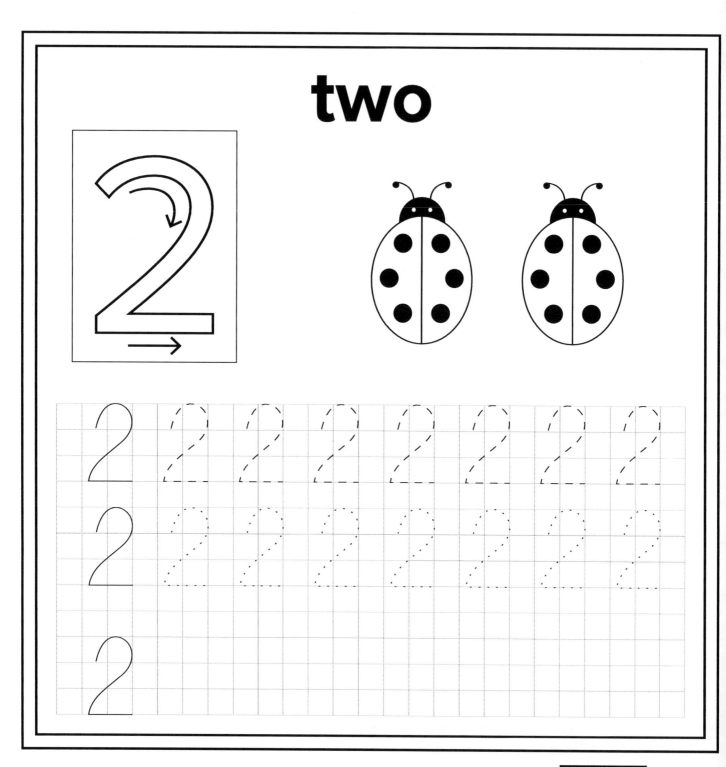

two

How many ladybirds?

three

3

How many hats?

four

How many mushrooms?

five

How many pears?

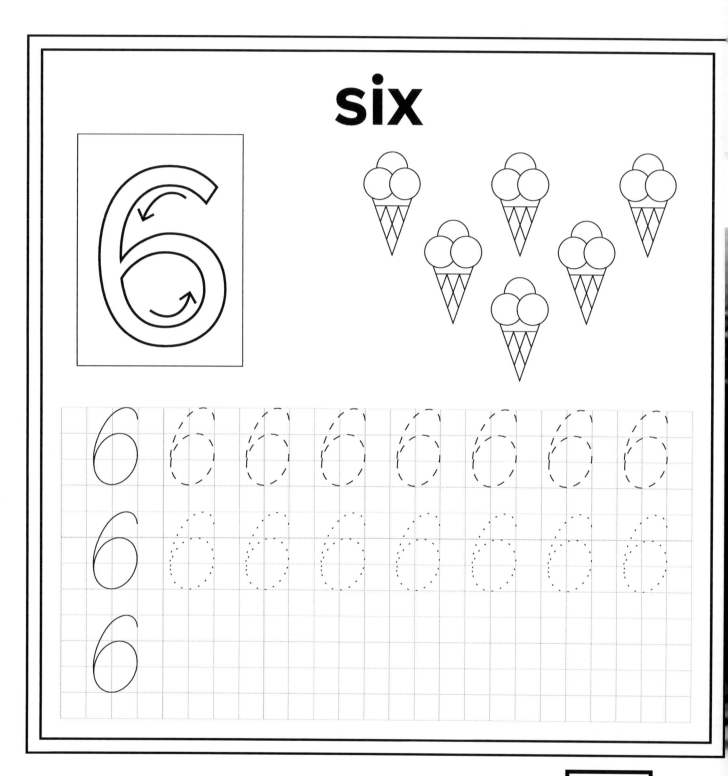

six

How many ice creams?

seven

How many snails?

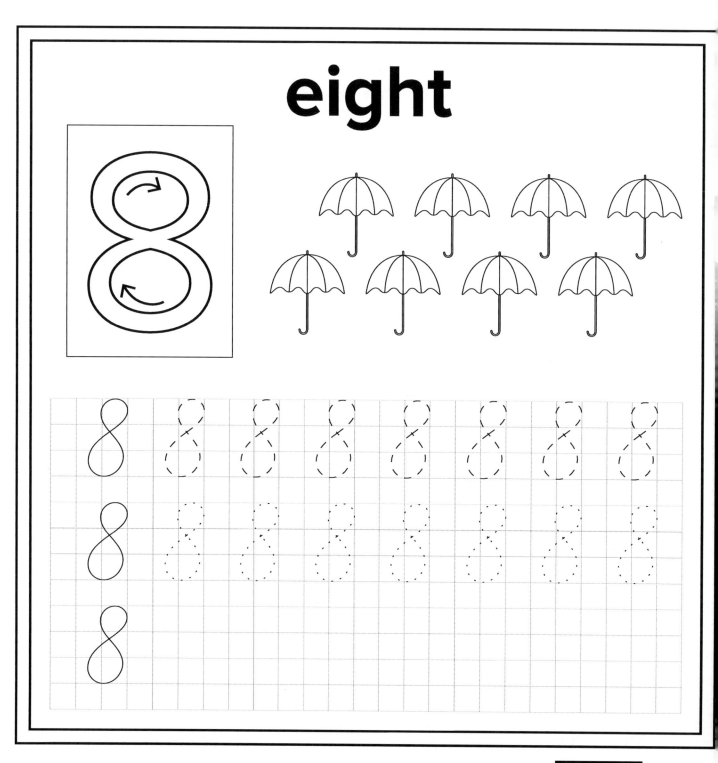

eight

How many umbrellas?

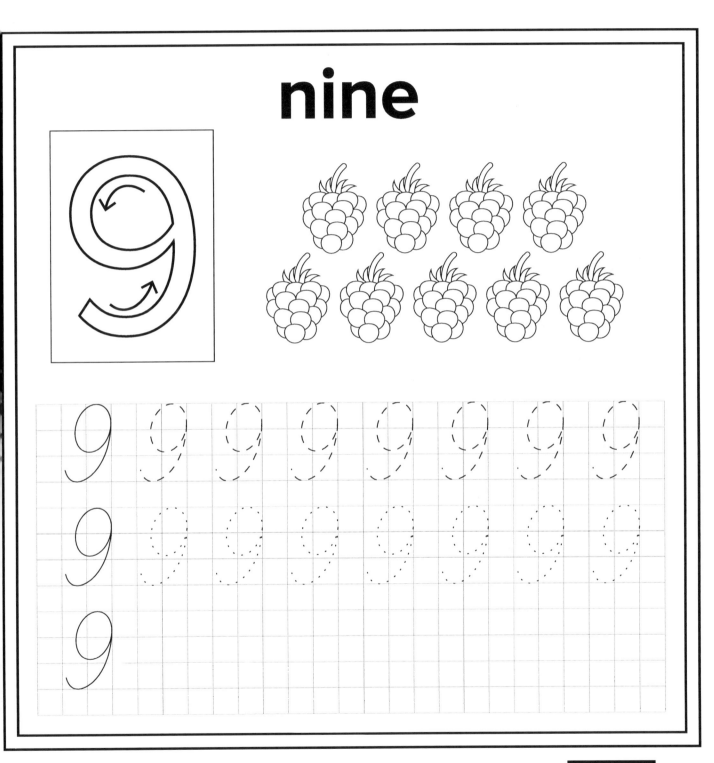

nine

How many raspberries?

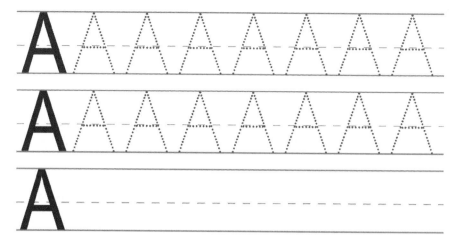

Find each letter A and colour the sections in **Green**

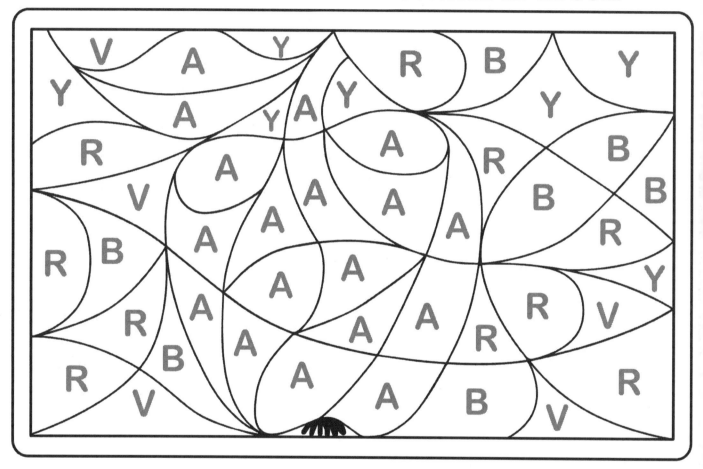

What is it?

....

B B B B B B B B B B
B B B B B B B B B B
B

Find each letter B and colour the sections in **light blue**

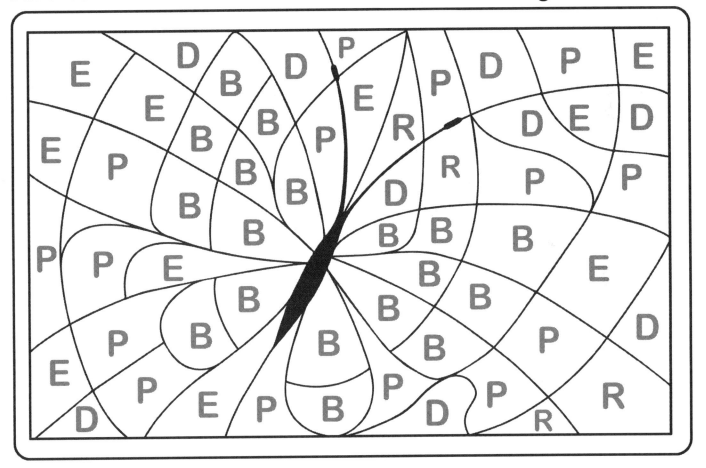

What is it?

....

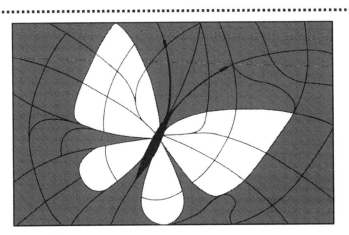

C C C C C C C C C

C C C C C C C C C

C

Find each letter C and colour the sections in **red**

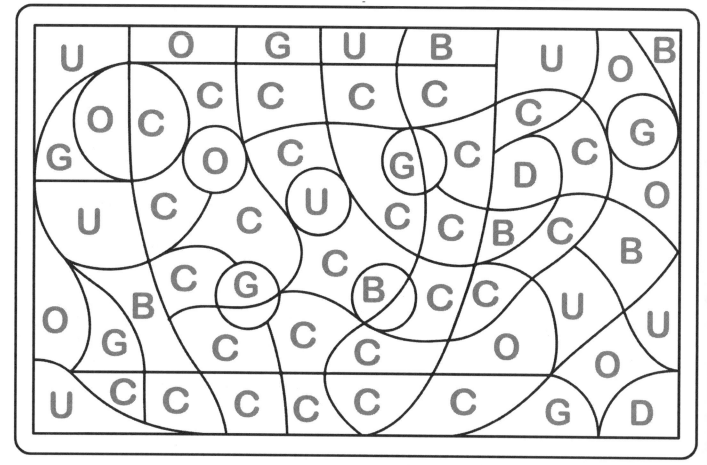

What is it?

....

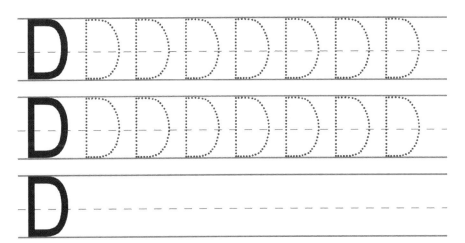

Find each letter D and colour the sections in **yellow**

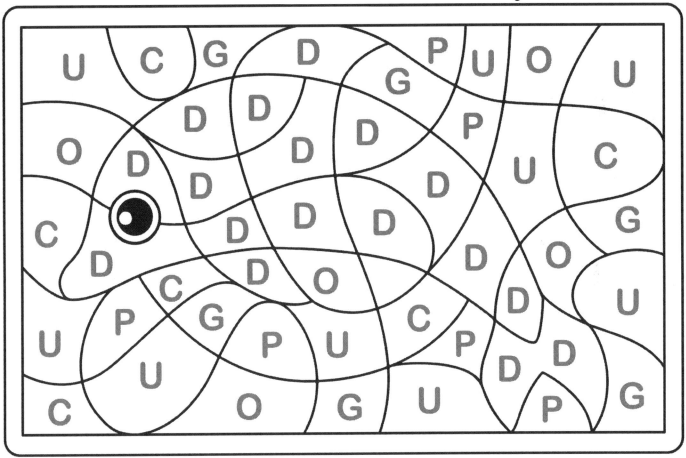

What is it?

....

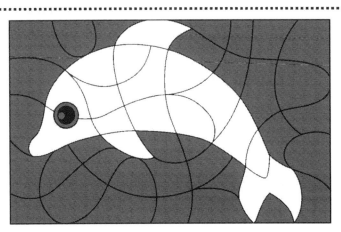

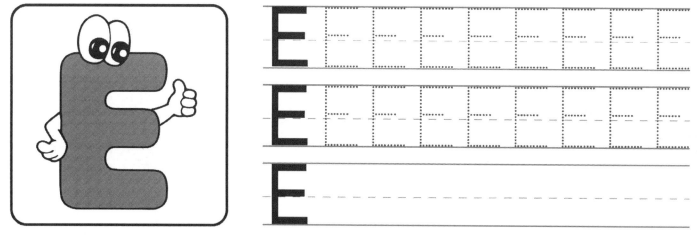

Find each letter E and colour the sections in **purple**

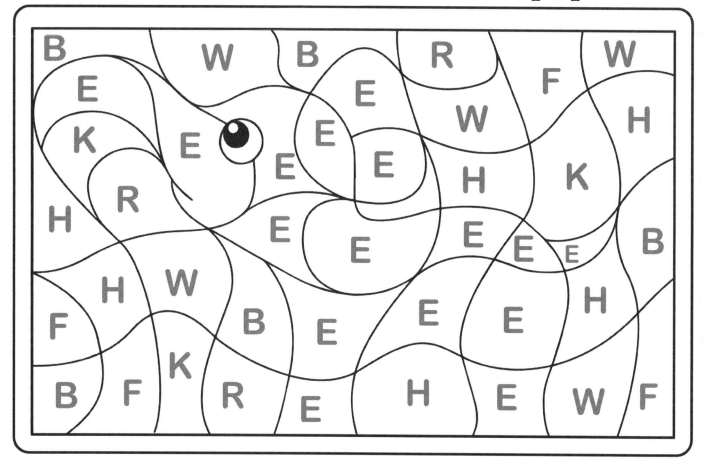

What is it?

....

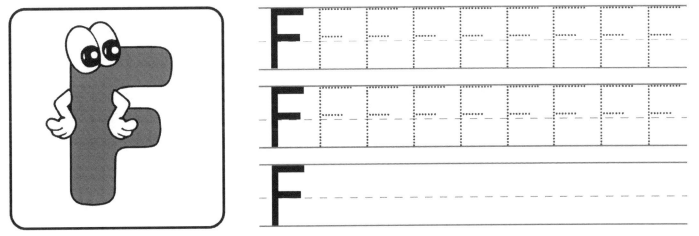

Find each letter F and colour the sections in **orange**

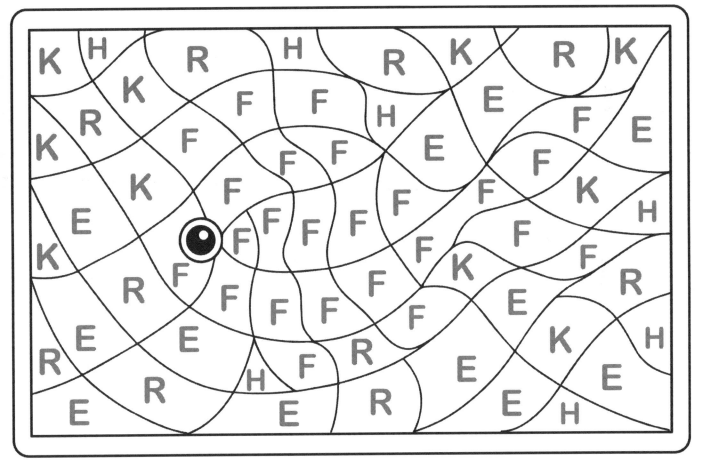

What is it?

....

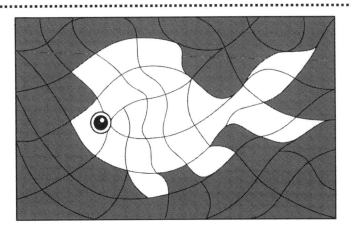

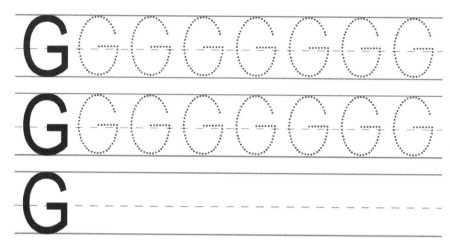

Find each letter G and colour the sections in **pink**

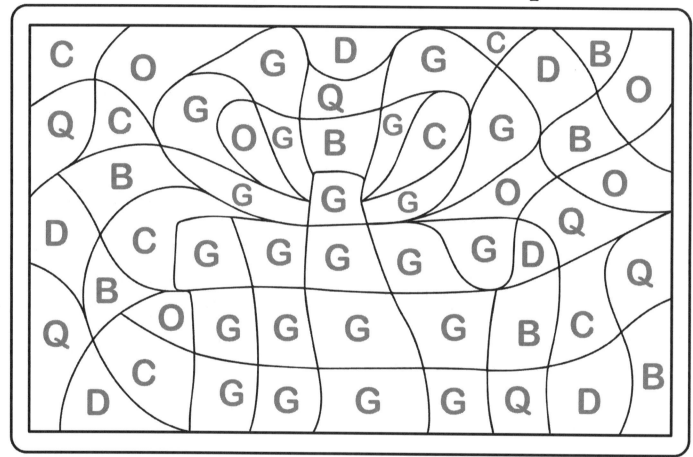

What is it?

....

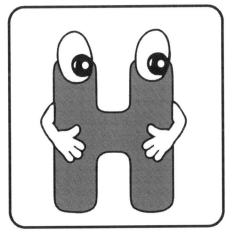

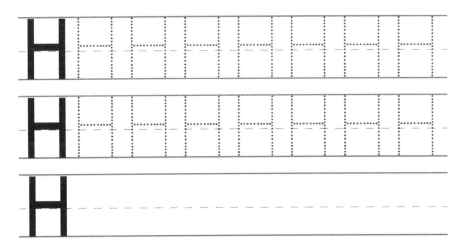

Find each letter H and colour the sections in **red**

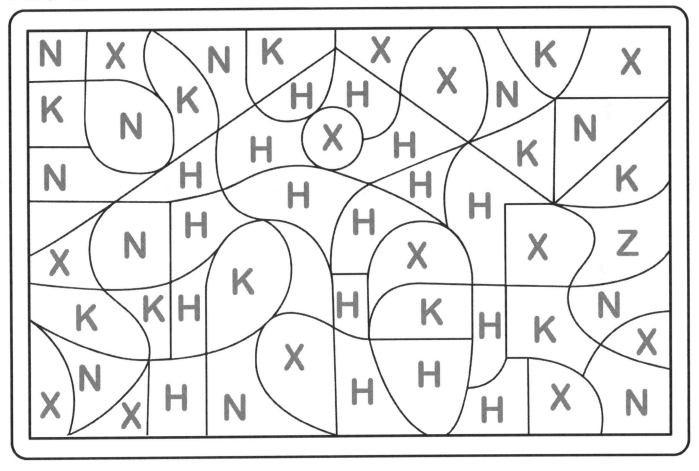

What is it?

....

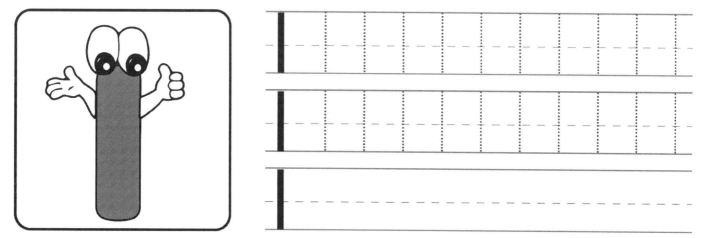

Find each letter I and colour the sections in **light green**

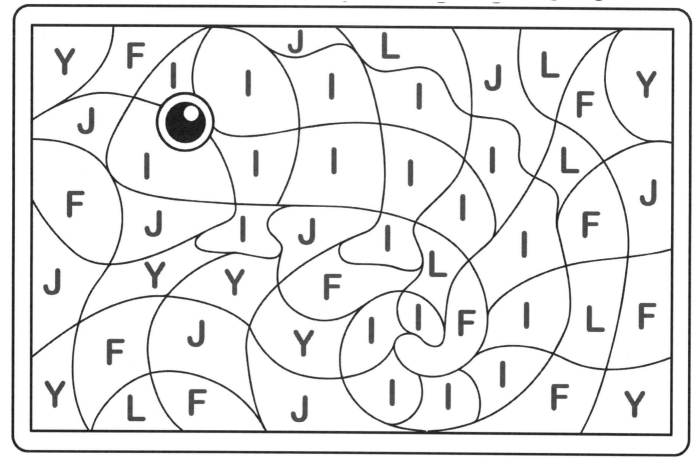

What is it?

....

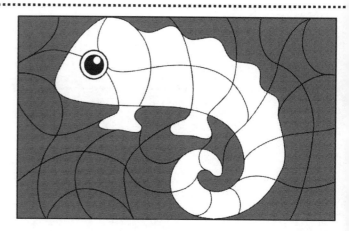

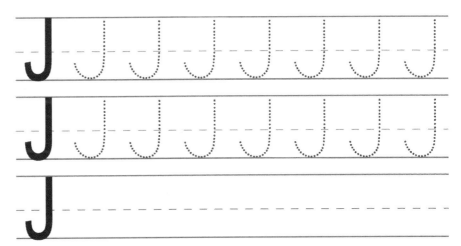

Find each letter J and colour the sections in **pink**

What is it?

....

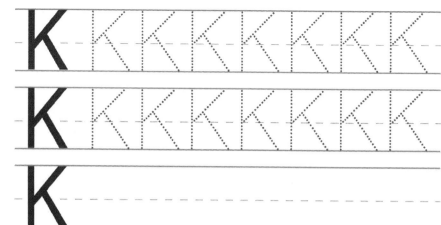

K

Find each letter K and colour the sections in **dark blue**

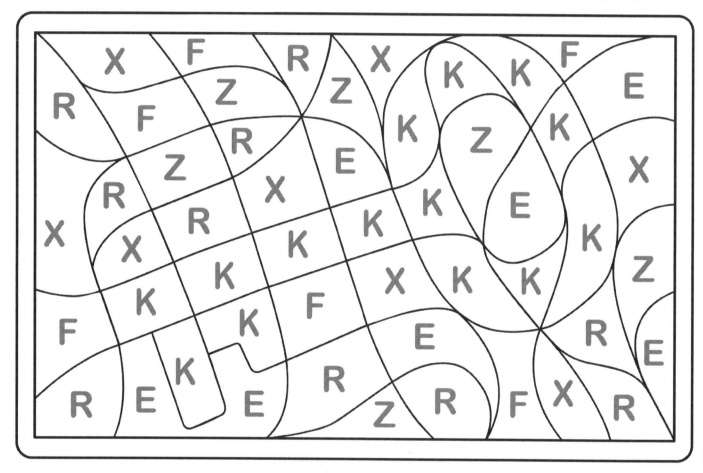

What is it?

....

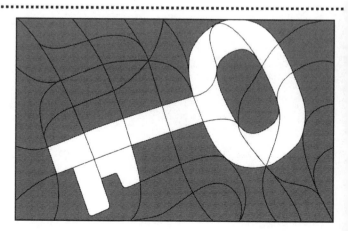

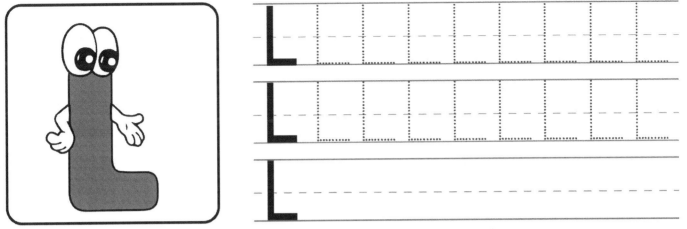

Find each letter L and colour the sections in **green**

What is it?

....

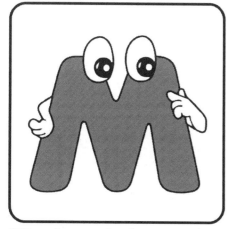

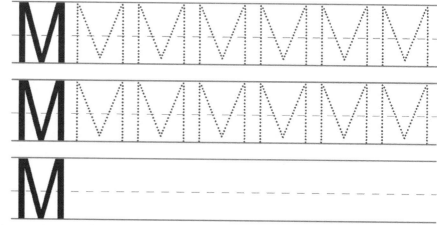

Find each letter M and colour the sections in **red**

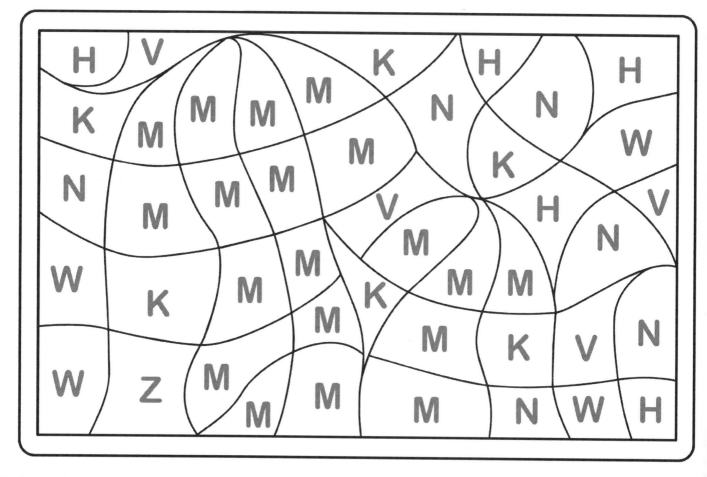

What is it?

....

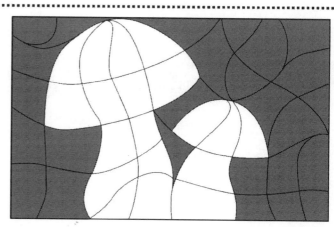

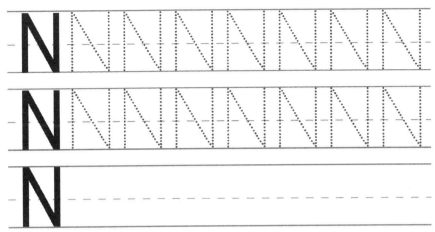

Find each letter N and colour the sections in **purple**

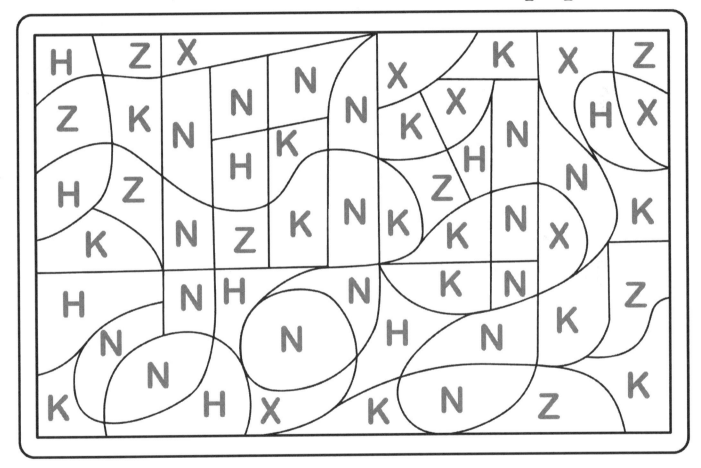

What is it?

....

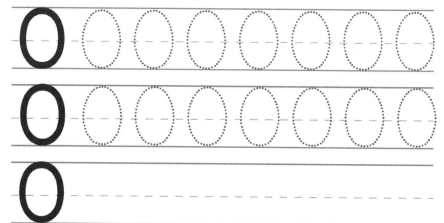

Find each letter O and colour the sections in **pink**

What is it?

....

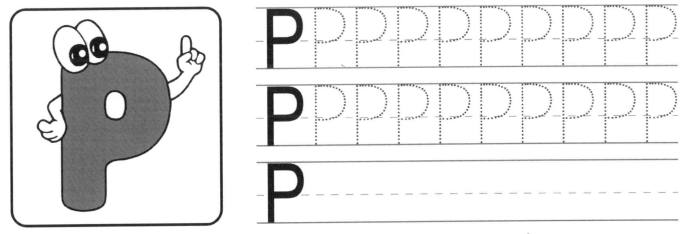

Find each letter P and colour the sections in **light green**

What is it?

....

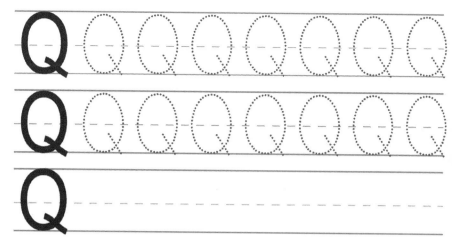

Find each letter Q and colour the sections in **yellow**

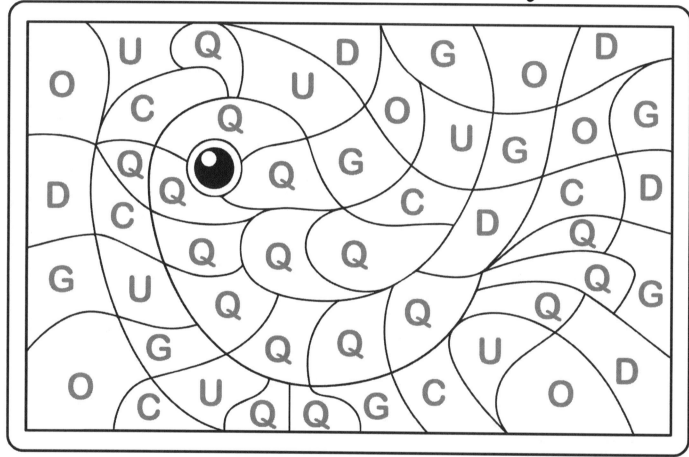

What is it?

....

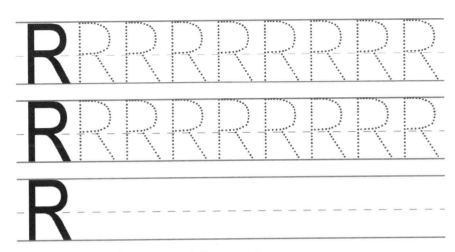

Find each letter R and colour the sections in **grey**

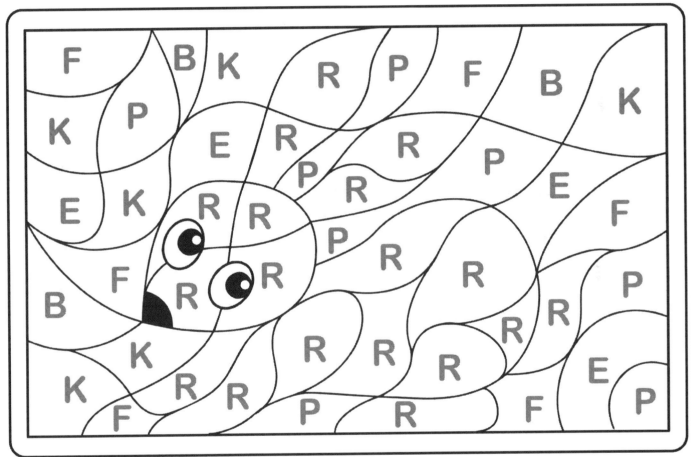

What is it?

....

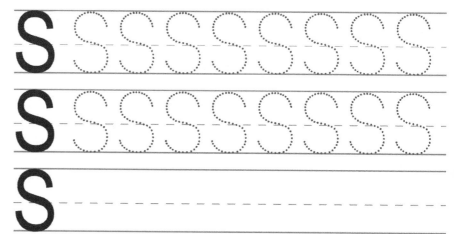

Find each letter S and colour the sections in **light green**

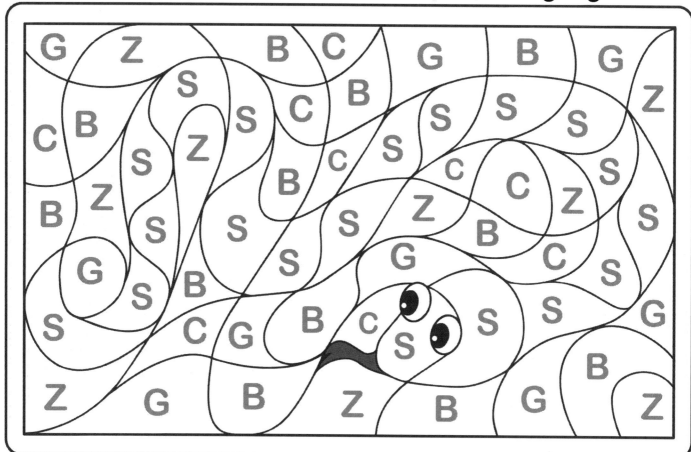

What is it?

....

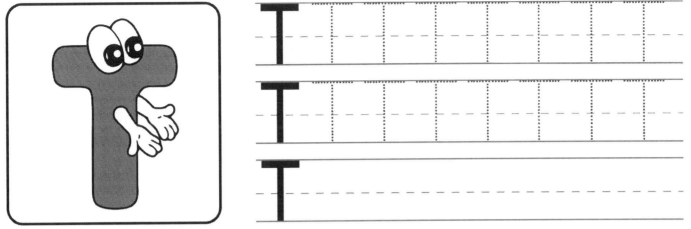

Find each letter T and colour the sections in **red**

What is it?

....

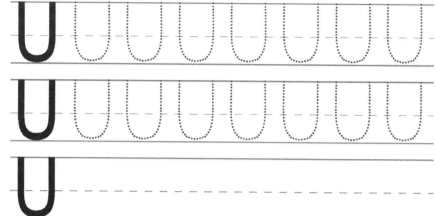

Find each letter U and colour the sections in **red**

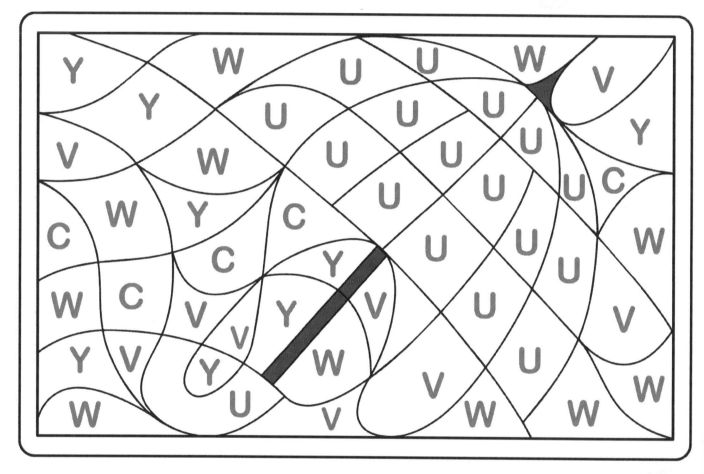

What is it?

....

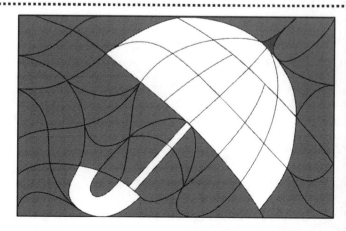

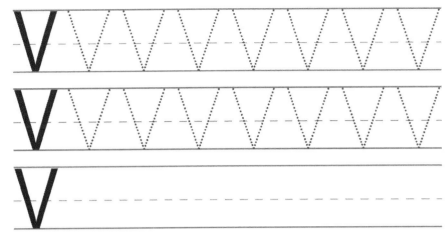

Find each letter V and colour the sections in **pink**

What is it?

....

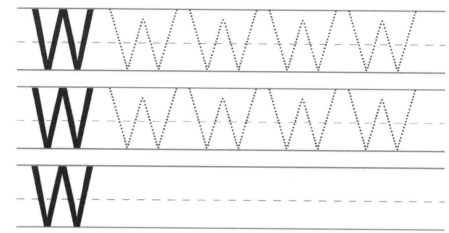

Find each letter W and colour the sections in **purple**

What is it?

....

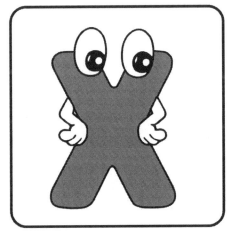

Find each letter X and colour the sections in **yellow**

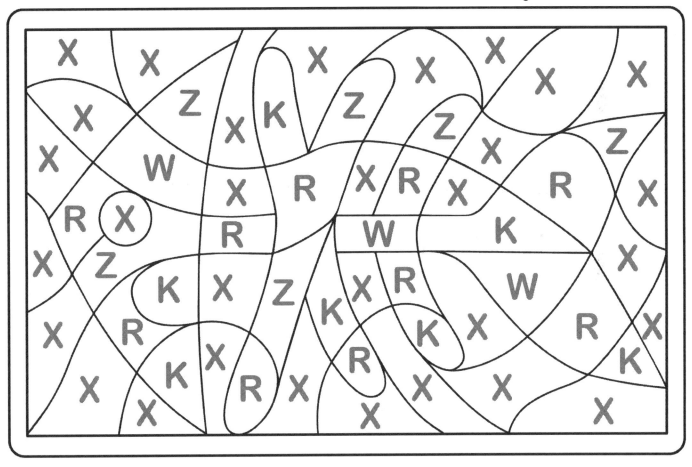

What is it?

....

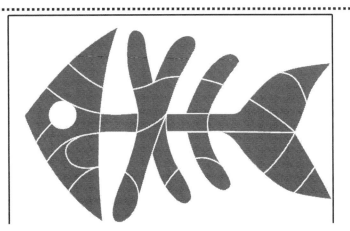

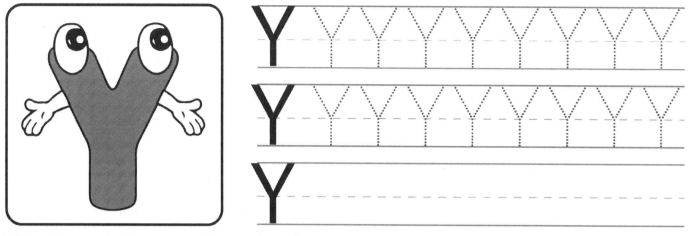

Find each letter Y and colour the sections in **blue**

What is it?

....

Z Z Z

Find each letter Z and colour the sections in **orange**

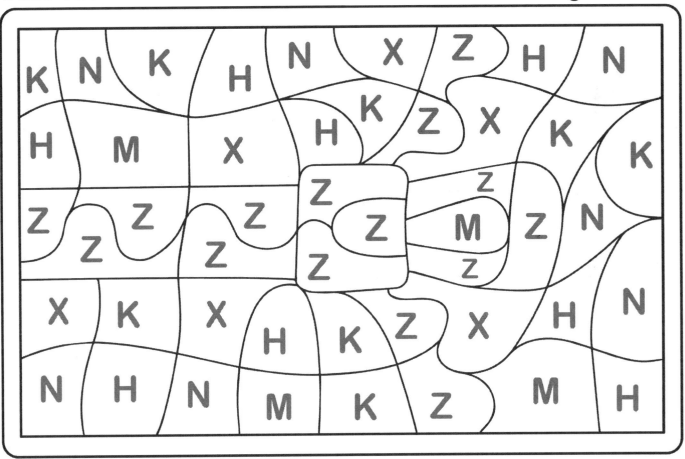

What is it?

....

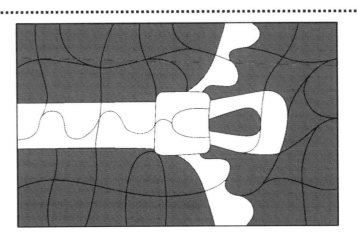